Romania

by Spencer Brinker

Consultant: Marjorie Faulstich Orellana, PhD
Professor of Urban Schooling
University of California, Los Angeles

BEARPORT PUBLISHING

New York, New York

Credits

Cover, © LordRunar/iStock and © Steve Debenport/iStock; TOC, © Sebastian Enache/Shutterstock; 4, © photosmatic/Shutterstock; 5T, © Lucian BOLCA/Shutterstock; 5B, © pathdoc/Shutterstock; 7, © Photografiero/Shutterstock; 8, © Inu/Shutterstock; 9T, © Catalin Lazar/Shutterstock; 9B, © Calin Stan/Shutterstock; 10, © Martin Pelanek/Shutterstock; 11T, © Tomas Hulik/Shutterstock; 11B, © MihaiDancaescu/Shutterstock; 12L, © sorincolac/iStock; 12–13, © radub85/iStock; 14T, © Bertrand Rieger/Hemis/Alamy; 14B, © Gabriel Petrescu/Shutterstock; 15T, © Ian 2010/Shutterstock; 15B, © Zharov Pavel/Shutterstock; 16, Public Domain; 17, © Remus Rigo/Alamy; 18, © warmcolors/iStock; 19T, Public Domain; 19B, Public Domain; 20, © Mykola Ivashchenko/Shutterstock; 21L, © Bruce Yuanyue Bi/Danita Delimont/Alamy; 21R, © Angyalosi Beata/Shutterstock; 22, © vkuslandia/Shutterstock; 23, © Danilova Janna/Shutterstock; 24, © Lucian BOLCA/Shutterstock; 25TL, © Balate Dorin/Shutterstock; 25TR, © Dziewul/Shutterstock; 25B, © Danilovski/Shutterstock; 26L, Public Domain; 26R, © Adriana Enache/Shutterstock; 27L, © Iain Masterton/Alamy; 27TR, © Valentin Armianu/Dreamstime; 27BR, © Christie's Images/Bridgeman Images; 28, © Cosminlftode/Shutterstock; 29L, © PhotoStock10/Shutterstock; 29R, © lev radin/Shutterstock; 30T, © Siempreverde22/Dreamstime and © Andreylobachev/Dreamstime; 30B, © Mihai Barbu/Reuters; 31 (T to B), © Calin Stan/Shutterstock, © Adam Petto/iStock, © marydan15/iStock, and © RossHelen/Shutterstock; 32, © nadi555/Shutterstock.

Publisher: Kenn Goin
Senior Editor: Joyce Tavolacci
Creative Director: Spencer Brinker
Design: Debrah Kaiser
Photo Researcher: Thomas Persano

Library of Congress Cataloging-in-Publication Data

Names: Brinker, Spencer, author.
Title: Romania / by Spencer Brinker.
Description: New York, New York : Bearport Publishing, 2019. | Series:
    Countries we come from | Includes bibliographical references and index.
Identifiers: LCCN 2018009259 (print) | LCCN 2018011049 (ebook) |
ISBN 9781684027378 (ebook) | ISBN 9781684026913 (library)
Subjects: LCSH: Romania—Juvenile literature.
Classification: LCC DR205 (ebook) | LCC DR205 .B75 2019 (print) |
DDC 949.8—dc23
LC record available at https://lccn.loc.gov/2018009259

For more information, write to Bearport Publishing Company, Inc., 45 West 21st Street, Suite 3B, New York, New York 10010. Printed in the United States of America.

10 9 8 7 6 5 4 3 2 1

Contents

Beautiful

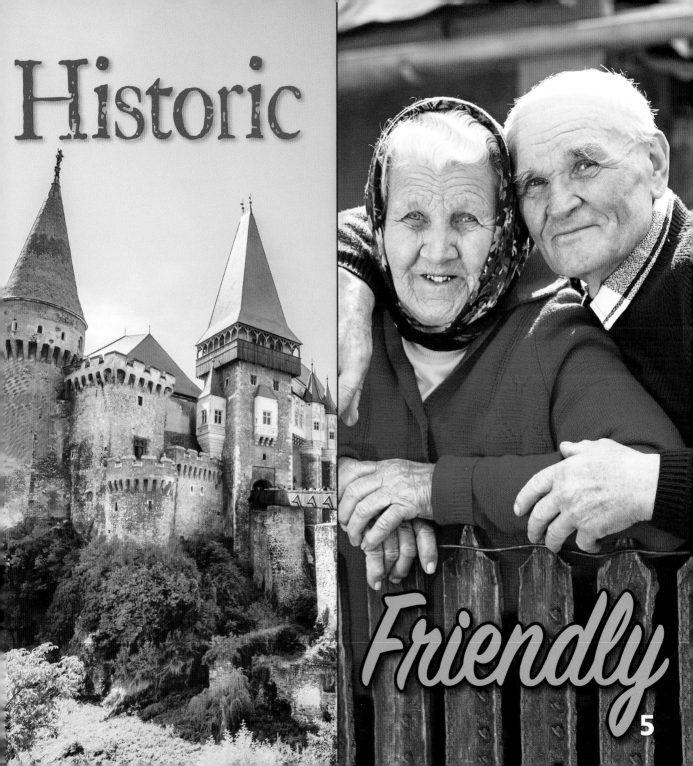

Historic

Friendly

5

Romania is a country in southeastern Europe.

It's about the same size as the state of Oregon.

EUROPE

Romania

Black Sea

Arctic Ocean

EUROPE

ASIA

Oregon

NORTH AMERICA

Atlantic Ocean

Pacific Ocean

Pacific Ocean

AFRICA

SOUTH AMERICA

Indian Ocean

AUSTRALIA

N

W   E

S

Southern Ocean

ANTARCTICA

Romania borders the Black Sea. The country is home to over 21 million people!

The landscape of Romania is beautiful.

There are tall, snowy mountains.

There are also thick forests and **majestic** waterfalls.

pelicans

The Danube **Delta** is where the Danube River empties into the Black Sea. It's home to 300 kinds of birds!

What animals live in Romania?

Chamois (SHAM-wah) are
a kind of goatlike antelope.

chamois

They climb
steep mountains.

Wildcats called lynx live in Romania, too.

They chase after the chamois!

The lynx is the national animal of Romania.

More brown bears live in Romania than in all of the rest of Europe!

Bucharest is Romania's largest city.

About two million people live there.

It's also the **capital** of the country.

Bucharest has many beautiful buildings and parks. As a result, it's called Little Paris!

13

In cities, Romanians have many jobs.

Some work in hotels and restaurants.

Others help construct new buildings.

In the countryside, lots of people work as farmers.

They grow wheat, potatoes, and sunflowers.

Farmers also raise sheep, goats, and chickens.

People have lived in Romania for thousands of years.

Different groups have controlled the land.

In the 1500s, the area was taken over by the Ottoman Empire.

The Ottoman Empire lasted from 1299 to 1923. It was based in Turkey and ruled huge areas of land.

Romania gained its **independence** in 1878.

Romania has many old castles, such as Bran Castle.

This is also known as Dracula's Castle!

Dracula is a famous story about a vampire.

The main character is Vlad Dracula.

He was named after a Romanian prince.

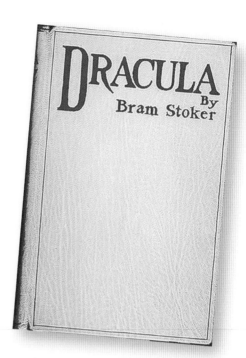

Prince Vlad Dracula, also know as Vlad the Impaler

Despite the stories, the real Prince Dracula probably didn't live in Bran Castle.

In Romania, most people speak Romanian.

This is how you say *hello*:

Buna (BOO-nah)

This is how you say *good-bye*:

La revedere
(LAH reh-veh-DEH-reh)

Prima Şcoală Românească
The First School in Romanian Language

Biserica Sf. Nicolae
The "Sf. Nicolae" Church

Zona de agrement Tâmpa
Walking Areas Tâmpa

Biserica Neagră
The Black Church

Casa Sfatului
The Council Hall

Centru

Hungarian is the second most common language in Romania.

What do Romanians enjoy eating?

Cabbage filled with meat and rice is a popular dish.

stuffed cabbage

Mamaliga (ma-MA-leeg-ah) is another favorite food.

It's made from boiled cornmeal.

Mamaliga is often served with salty cheese or rich sour cream. *Yum!*

About 80 percent of Romanians are Christian.

They worship in churches.

The tallest wooden church in the world is in Romania.

Some churches are covered with paintings!

The Merry Cemetery has hundreds of colorful gravestones.

Many great artists come from Romania.

Constantin Brâncuși is one of the most famous.

He's known for creating graceful sculptures.

Constantin Brâncuși

One of Brâncuși's most famous works is called *The Kiss*.

This artwork is called *The Prayer*.

What sports do Romanians love?

Soccer!

Basketball and tennis are also popular.

Romania is known for its excellent gymnasts, too.

Romanian Nadia Comăneci was the first Olympic gymnast to get a perfect score!

29

Fast Facts

Capital city: Bucharest

Population of Romania: Over 21 million

Main language: Romanian

Money: Romanian Leu*

Major religion: Christianity

Neighboring countries include: Ukraine, Moldova, Bulgaria, Serbia, and Hungary

*Romania became part of the European Union in 2007. Around 2022, the country will switch its currency to the Euro.

Cool Fact: Was baseball invented in Romania? *Oina* (OYN–yah) is a Romanian sport that's played with a stick and a ball. It's 600 years old!

capital (KAP-uh-tuhl) a city where a country's government is based

delta (DEL-tuh) a piece of land formed by sand and mud at the end of a river

independence (in-di-PEN-dunce) freedom from outside control

majestic (muh-JES-tik) grand and beautiful

31

Index

Read More

Goldberg, Enid A, and Norman Itzkowitz. *Vlad the Impaler: The Real Count Dracula (A Wicked History).* New York: Scholastic (2009).

Sheehan, Sean. *Romania (Cultures of the World).* Tarrytown, NY: Benchmark (2005).

Learn More Online

To learn more about Romania, visit
www.bearportpublishing.com/CountriesWeComeFrom

About the Author

Spencer Brinker lives and works in New York City.
He has met many amazing Romanian people,
and he hopes to visit the beautiful country one day.